contents

Key

- Number and Place value
- Addition and Subtraction
- Multiplication and Division
- Shape, Data, Probability and Measure
- Fractions and Decimals
- Algebra
- Mixed Operations

How to use this book

The first page of each section will have a title telling you what the next few pages are about.

Read the instructions carefully before each set of questions.

Some pages will show you an example or model.

Sometimes a character will give you a tip.

Dividing 4-digit numbers by 2-digit numbers

Write out the times table answers for the divisor to help you.

Use long division to solve these problems.

```
5836 ÷ 24 = ☐
        200 + 40 + 3, r4
   24 ) 5836
      – 4800
         1036
        –  960
           76
         –  72
            4
```

24	144
48	168
72	192
96	216
120	240

1 3699 ÷ 24 = ☐   4 4578 ÷ 32 = ☐   7 5876 ÷ 23 = ☐
2 6742 ÷ 31 = ☐   5 2465 ÷ 22 = ☐   8 8764 ÷ 26 = ☐
3 4678 ÷ 23 = ☐   6 6487 ÷ 31 = ☐   9 4445 ÷ 22 = ☐

10 Bottles in a factory are packed into crates that hold 24 bottles. How many crates are needed to hold 3699 bottles?

11 A company must supply at least 4658 flashcards to a distributor in 32 days' time. The machine that makes the flashcards is programmed to make the same whole number each day. How many should it be programmed for?

12 A shop buys jackets for £26. How many of them can they buy with £1745?

THINK If a whole number ending in 0 is divided by a 2-digit number ending in 2, the answer never has a remainder. Is this true? Try some divisions to find out.

● I am confident with using long division to divide 4-digit numbers.

38

Set out these problems and solve them using long division.

1 2563 ÷ 33 = ☐   6 7253 ÷ 24 = ☐   11 4024 ÷ 27 = ☐

2 5783 ÷ 27 = ☐   7 6234 ÷ 42 = ☐   12 7255 ÷ 24 = ☐

3 5353 ÷ 34 = ☐   8 7426 ÷ 26 = ☐   13 6666 ÷ 34 = ☐

4 6463 ÷ 42 = ☐   9 3068 ÷ 27 = ☐   14 2652 ÷ 27 = ☐

5 2856 ÷ 33 = ☐   10 9321 ÷ 33 = ☐   15 9678 ÷ 42 = ☐

16 A company must supply at least 4024 batteries to a distributor in 27 days' time. The machine that makes the batteries is programmed to make the same whole number each day. How many should it be programmed for?

17 A craftsman wants to make 1646 wooden bowls over the next two years. How many bowls should he aim to make each month?

18 A shop buys mobile phones for £42. How many of them can they buy with £1745?

19 In a chocolate factory individual chocolates are put into boxes of 26. How many boxes can be filled with 3643 chocolates?

THINK 3001 is divided by an odd number and has a remainder of 5. What is the answer?

● I am confident with using long division to divide 4-digit numbers.

39

THINK questions will challenge you to think more about the maths on the page.

Each area of maths has its own colour.

Choose a traffic light colour to say how confident you are with the maths on the page.

7-digit numbers

Write each set of numbers in order.

1. 34 567   21 738   78 210

2. 123 431   146 379   203 483

3. 7 643 245   4 321 709   7 124 976

Answer these questions.

4. Write a number that comes between 30 000 and 40 000.

5. Write a number that comes between 300 000 and 400 000.

6. Write a number that comes between 3 000 000 and 4 000 000.

7. Use each of the digits 3, 4 and 5 once, to make this true:

$$\boxed{}\,2\,\boxed{}\,36 > \boxed{}\,4917$$

Write the next two numbers in each sequence.

8. 7 652 996, 7 652 997, 7 652 998, ☐, ☐

9. 2430, 2420, 2410, ☐, ☐

10. 15 895, 15 900, 15 905, 15 910, ☐, ☐

THINK How many 7-digit numbers can you write, where each digit is one less than the digit to its left?

● I am confident with reading, writing and
○
○ ordering 7-digit numbers.
○

Use the number cards to complete the inequalities.

| 2 | 3 | 5 | 7 | q |

1 4 37 ☐ 1 ☐ ☐ < ☐ 816 0 ☐ q

2 8 ☐ 3 ☐ 087 < 85 ☐ ☐ 2 ☐ 1

3 76 ☐ 2 ☐ 71 < 7 65 ☐ 6 ☐ ☐

Use the digits 1–7 to make a number between:

4 3 000 000 and 4 000 000

5 2 500 000 and 3 000 000

6 6 400 000 and 6 500 000

Write each set of numbers in order.

7 639 820   472 q11   651 207   425 710

8 4 876 024   8 217 3q0   4 510 246   5 217 6q2

q 27 5q4   18 361   45 q86   54 233

Choose a number between 7 qqq qq4 and 7 qqq qqq.
Add 8 to your number. Can your partner work out
what your original number was?

● I am confident with reading, writing and
○ ordering 7-digit numbers.

Write each set of numbers in order.

① 3 456 213   3 124 678   3 045 678   3 029 134

② 746 201   764 327   663 109   746 213

③ 2 780 125   2 786 521   2 792 431   2 782 478

Use the number cards to complete the questions.

| 4 | 7 | 9 | 8 | 1 | 0 |

④ Use each card twice to complete this inequality.

☐☐☐☐☐☐ < ☐☐☐☐☐☐

⑤ Now use each card once to make a number as close to 500 000 as possible.

⑥ Use each card once to complete this inequality.

6 35☐☐2☐ < 63☐1☐2☐

Decide if each statement is true or false.

⑦ There are ten 7-digit numbers where the digits are all the same.

⑧ The smallest 7-digit number with three '9's as digits is bigger than one million plus one thousand.

⑨ The largest 6-digit number is only 1 less than the smallest 7-digit number.

⑩ If neither number has a '0' in it, the largest 5-digit number is 11 112 smaller than the smallest 6-digit number.

I am confident with reading, writing and ordering 7-digit numbers.

Decimal place value

1 Using only these digits, complete this number sentence.

| 1 | 3 | 4 |

2▢·▢▢   <   21·43

2 Using only these digits, complete this number sentence.

| 5 | 0 | 3 | 6 | 1 |

7▢·▢▢   >   7▢·▢4

3 Match each decimal number with its pair. Write down the pairs.

| 0·03 | $\frac{1}{4}$ | 0·7 | $\frac{47}{100}$ | 0·25 | $\frac{7}{10}$ | $\frac{3}{100}$ | 0·47 |

Round each of these values to the nearest whole number.

4 6·01   **5** 9·51   **6** 7·75

7 Write down the two fractions that are equivalent to 0·6.

$\frac{6}{10}$ $\frac{1}{60}$ $\frac{60}{100}$ $\frac{1}{6}$

THINK Write two decimal numbers less than 1. One number should be a 3-place decimal and the other should be a 2-place decimal. The two numbers can only differ by 0·001.

● I am confident with reading, writing and ordering
○
○ decimal numbers.

Round each number to the nearest tenth and then to the nearest whole number.

3·57 ⟶ 3·6 ⟶ 4

1. 2·83 ⟶ 2·☐ ⟶ ☐
2. 7·51 ⟶ ☐ ⟶ ☐
3. 5·32 ⟶ ☐ ⟶ ☐

Now solve these questions.

4. Write these values in order, from the smallest to the largest.

$\frac{63}{100}$ 0·06   0·62 $\frac{1}{6}$ 0·16

5. Copy and complete this number line.

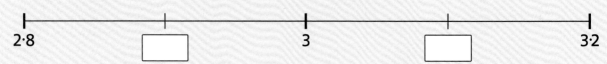

2·8 ———— ☐ ———— 3 ———— ☐ ———— 3·2

6. Copy this number line and put the number cards in the right place.

4·25 ———————————————————— 4·75 | 4·5 | 4·65 |

Write fractions equivalent to these decimals.

7. 0·3   9. 0·125   11. 0·271

8. 0·7   10. 0·36   12. 0·313

 Write a 1-place decimal number and a 3-place decimal number with the smallest possible difference. Both numbers must be less than 1.

I am confident with reading, writing and ordering decimal numbers.

Multiplying and dividing by 10, 100 and 1000

Use place-value to help you solve these problems.

320 ÷ 100 = 3·2

10 000s	1000s	100s	10s	1s	•	0·1s	0·01s
		3	2	0			
				3	•	2	

1. 45 × 1000 = ☐

2. 265 × 10 = ☐

3. 2·7 × 100 = ☐

4. $\frac{1}{10}$ of 7 = ☐

5. 9·7 × 100 = ☐

6. 47·3 ÷ 10 = ☐

7. 872 × 100 = ☐

8. 0·14 × 100 = ☐

9. 18 ÷ 10 = ☐

10. 26 150 ÷ 100 = ☐

11. 64 ÷ 100 = ☐

12. 13 700 ÷ 1000 = ☐

THINK If a 5-digit whole number with five non-zero digits is divided by 10 000, how many decimal places does it have?

● I am confident with multiplying and dividing by 10,
○ 100 and 1000 using place value.
○

Multiply each number by 10.

1 26·38   **2** 472   **3** 9·17   **4** 16 352

Divide each number by 10.

5 26·4   **6** 296   **7** 8·2   **8** 72·85

Multiply each number by 100.

9 6·19   **10** 9327   **11** 0·35   **12** 854

Divide each number by 100.

13 28·7   **14** 16 582   **15** 781   **16** 4603

Find a tenth of:

17 43   **18** 820   **19** 15   **20** 1580

 A 2-place decimal number less than 1 is multiplied by 100 000. There must be four digits in the answer. Is this true or false?

I am confident with multiplying and dividing by 10, 100 and 1000 using place value.

Rounding numbers

Copy and complete these tables.

1

	Round to nearest 10	Round to nearest 100	Round to nearest 1000	Round to nearest 10 000
5 452 876				
372 561				
7 408 396				
85 724				
576 055				

2

	Round to nearest 1	Round to nearest 0·1	Round to nearest 0·01
16·573			
28·914			
1·702			
34·567			
12·048			

3 Write three numbers that will round to 7 000 000, if you are rounding to the nearest million.

 **THINK** A 2-place decimal number rounds to 3 as the nearest whole number. A second 2-place decimal rounds to 4 as the nearest whole number. How close together could these numbers be?

I am confident with rounding both 7-digit numbers and 3-place decimals.

Positive and negative numbers

Write these numbers in order from smallest to largest.

1. −7   −17   −7·7   1·7   27

2. −48   12   53   −9   −2·1

Add 5 to each of these numbers.

3. −6 ⟶ ☐   4. −12 ⟶ ☐   5. −3 ⟶ ☐

Now answer these questions.

6. The temperature in the Arctic Circle is 30 °C colder at night. If it reaches 12 °C in the day, how cold is it at night?

7. Look at the thermometers. What is the difference between the two recorded temperatures?

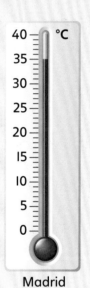

Madrid

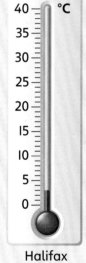

Halifax

8. Copy this number line and mark on −5 and −9.

```
├──────────────────────────────┼──────────────┤
−10                            0              5
```

During one 24-hour day, the minimum and maximum temperatures in a city are 20 °C apart. If the minimum is between 0 °C and −4 °C, what are the possible whole number maximum temperatures?

I am confident with reading, writing and ordering negative numbers.

Write each set of numbers in order from smallest to largest.

1 −27 5 −28 13 26 −5

2 −1 −0·5 0·5 0 1·5 −1·5

Use these cards to write pairs of numbers with a difference of one.

3

| −12·8 | −11·4 | −11·8 | −13·5 | −12·4 | −14·5 |

Now solve these problems.

4 The temperature inside an aeroplane is 22 °C. Outside the aeroplane it is −30 °C. What is the difference between these two temperatures?

5 What is the difference between the temperatures on these thermometers?

6 The two tag numbers have a difference of 20 °C. Write two possible pairs of numbers that they could be.

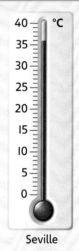

Seville   Lancaster

```
├────────────┬─────────────────┬──────────────┤
−20          □        0         □            20
```

7 Draw this line and mark on −0·45 and 1·5.

```
├┼┼┼┼┼┼┼┼┼┼┼┼┼┼┼┼┼┼┼┼┼┼┼┼┼┼┼┼┼┼┼┤
−2                 0                 2
```

 The temperature difference between midday and midnight in Albany is 12 degrees. The daytime temperature varies between 18 °C and 24 °C. Write some possible temperatures at midnight and midday.

● ○ ○ **I am confident with reading, writing and ordering negative numbers.**

13

Copy these number lines and mark –7 on each of them.

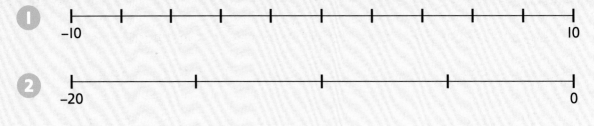

1

–10   10

2

–20   0

3

–13   0   5

Now solve these problems.

Each player loses 50 points when they land on a penalty in a computer game. Work out their scores now if their scores before getting the penalty were:

4 Sam, 268

6 Jack, 24

8 Ayesha, 31

5 Sarah, 314

7 Min, 18

9 Krysia, 49

10 The daytime temperature in Denver is 25 °C. It drops to –4 °C at night. What is the difference between these two temperatures?

THINK What realistic temperatures could London have during a summer's day if the minimum and maximum temperatures during a 24-hour period have a difference of 10 °C?

● I am confident with reading, writing and ordering
○ negative numbers.
○

Adding and subtracting whole numbers and decimals

Copy and complete these additions and subtractions.

1. 271 + 824 = ☐

2. ☐ + 952 = 1852

3. 26 300 − 14 250 = ☐

4. 8615 − 2763 = ☐

5. 16 528 − 7999 = ☐

6. 27 298 + 16 597 = ☐

7. 7595 − ☐ = 3525

8. 37 + 46 + 85 + 78 = ☐

Now solve these word problems.

9. Year 6's leaving celebration is to go to an adventure park. For the whole class to go it will cost £478·20. The class have raised £284·60 so far. How much more do they need to raise to afford the trip?

10. James has £8956 in his savings account. He wants to buy a new large-screen TV that costs £3999. How much money would he have left if he did buy it?

11. A fish-and-chip shop made profits of £15 300 last year. This year they made profits that were £6553 more than last year. What were their profits this year? What were their total profits for the two years?

20 588 − 19 301

THINK

This could be solved mentally or by using a written method. Discuss with a partner which method would be easier and why.

○ **I am confident with adding and subtracting numbers**
○ **with up to 5-digits.**
○

15

Copy and complete these additions and subtractions.

1. $219 + \boxed{} = 345$

2. $67\,423 - 28\,416 = \boxed{}$

3. $12\,406 + \boxed{} = 17\,498$

4. $8429 + 34\,966 = \boxed{}$

5. $10\,000 - 9417 = \boxed{}$

6. $476 - 298 = \boxed{}$

7. $721 + 63 + 490 = \boxed{}$

8. $81\,307 - 15\,999 = \boxed{}$

9. $346\,297 + 154\,832 = \boxed{}$

10. $3\,498\,250 + 2\,200\,409 = \boxed{}$

Now solve these word problems.

11. Anna, Anouska and Taylor are raising money for charity by doing a sponsored walk. Anouska raises £3·80 more than Taylor. Anna collects £25. Taylor collects £13·00 less than Anna. Altogether, how much money have the children raised?

12. In a weekly TV talent show there are three contestants left. This week Ayla got 18 795 votes, Oli got 9 799 votes and Fi got 1001 votes more than Oli. How many votes were there altogether and how many more votes than Fi did Ayla get?

THINK Write a subtraction for your partner which could be easily solved either mentally or by using a written method. Discuss why it could be done either way.

○ **I am confident with adding and subtracting numbers with up to 7-digits.**

Solve these word problems.

1 Small green apples are 25p each. Large red apples are 37p each. David has £2·50 to spend. How many small green apples can he buy for this amount? How many large red apples can he buy?

2 Caitlyn and Evie enter the long jump on sports day. Caitlyn jumps 2 metres 58 centimetres but Evie jumps 16 centimetres more! How long was Evie's jump in metres?

3 Ibraheem and Charlotte have some sweets. Altogether they have 26 sweets. Ibraheem has two more than Charlotte. How many sweets have they each got?

4 I have a piece of string that is 3·4 m long. I cut off a piece 63 cm long. How much string remains?

5 A seed begins to grow. After two days the shoot is 2·2 cm tall. It grows a further 8 mm each day for the next three days. How tall is it now?

6 Three items weigh 2 kg, 395 g and 0·75 kg. What is the total mass of the three items?

7 What number lies half-way between 4828 and 5032?

THINK Write a subtraction where using the column subtraction method will mean that you have to move four digits across, but using Frog will mean only three jumps.

I am confident with adding and subtracting numbers in word problems.

Use place value to solve these.

1 $20·61 + 30·07 = \boxed{}$

2 $35·28 - 23·16 = \boxed{}$

3 $13·58 + 6·31 = \boxed{}$

4 $14·54 + 3·21 = \boxed{}$

5 $7·84 - 3·22 = \boxed{}$

6 $27·96 + 13·62 = \boxed{}$

Use rounding to solve these.

7 $49·63 - 31·99 = \boxed{}$

8 $12·87 - 4·99 = \boxed{}$

9 $67·77 + 6·99 = \boxed{}$

10 $26·38 + 15·99 = \boxed{}$

11 $70·44 + 8·98 = \boxed{}$

12 $61·23 - 5·95 = \boxed{}$

Use column addition or Frog to answer these.

13 $19 + 8·76 + 13·29 = \boxed{}$

14 $44·83 - 37·66 = \boxed{}$

15 $35·56 + 27·78 = \boxed{}$

16 $17·58 + 24·65 + 6·46 = \boxed{}$

17 $374·8 - 285·4 = \boxed{}$

18 $125·9 + 48·75 = \boxed{}$

 Write an addition which you can use rounding to solve. Give it to a partner to work out.

I am confident with using different methods to solve decimal addition and subtraction.

Solve these problems.

1 73·86 + 135·72 = ☐   **3** 8·5 – 2·69 = ☐

2 9·6 – 3·75 = ☐   **4** 68·37 + 164·78 = ☐

Answer these questions.

5 Write the two numbers that have a difference of 0·5.

0·7   0·75   0·25   0·6   0·65

6 Write the two numbers that have a difference of 2.

0·2   –1·2   –2   4   –2·2   0·8

Now solve these word problems.

7 A jug of squash holds 2·5 l. Each glass can hold 0·35 l. Marios fills three glasses. How much squash is left in the jug?

8 A male African elephant is 3·6 m tall. A female elephant is 0·72 m shorter. How tall is she?

9 One parcel weighs 1·8 kg. Another weighs 0·27 kg less. How much do they weigh in total?

10 A car is driving at a speed of 46·4 km per hour. It slows its speed down by 0·65 km per hour and then speeds up to go 11·3 km per hour faster. How fast is it going now?

 Copy and complete this problem. Fill in the missing digits.

$$
\begin{array}{r}
\boxed{}\,\boxed{}\,\cdot\,\boxed{}\,\boxed{} \\
+\quad \boxed{}\,6\,\cdot\,5\,6 \\
\hline
6\,4\,\cdot\,7\,1
\end{array}
$$

Fractions and percentages

Find each percentage.

1. 50% of 180

2. 10% of 220

3. 25% of 400

4. 90% of 200

Write the smaller amount as a percentage of the larger amount.

5. 60 of 240

6. 800 of 8000

7. 6 of 30

8. 5·5 of 27·5

Write these fractions as percentages.

9. $\frac{1}{10}$

10. $\frac{3}{4}$

11. $\frac{1}{4}$

12. $\frac{1}{5}$

Now solve these word problems.

13. A pair of jeans cost £25. In a sale they are reduced by 10%. How much do they cost in the sale?

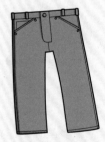

14. Cinema tickets are £12 each. On a Wednesday the tickets cost 25% less. Kath and Ron go together to see a film. How much do their tickets cost in total?

15. There are 3000 people at a rugby match. 10% of them are children and the rest are adults. 20% of the adults are women. How many children are there? How many of the adults are women? How many of the adults are men?

○ **I am confident with converting and calculating**
○ **percentages.**
○

Find each percentage.

1 50% of 390

3 90% of 2860

2 20% of 760

4 15% of 500

Write each smaller amount as a percentage of the larger amount.

5 75 of 375

7 820 of 16 400

6 26 of 520

8 3·5 of 28

Write these fractions as percentages.

9 $\frac{24}{32}$

11 $\frac{15}{120}$

10 $\frac{16}{64}$

12 $\frac{7}{20}$

Now solve these word problems.

13 Kevin wants to buy a game for his console. It costs £43·50 normally but has been reduced by 20%. How much will it cost now?

14 A weekend break to France costs £358. The holiday company is reducing the cost by 15%. What is the new price?

15 Find the difference between £650 reduced by 50% and £560 reduced by 60%.

16 Last week a TV soap opera had 7545 viewers. This week it had 20% fewer viewers. How many viewers did it have this week?

I am confident with converting and calculating percentages.

Algebra

Remember to check if the brackets will change the calculation order.

Solve these problems.

1. $(8 + 3) \times 9 = \square$

2. $8 + (3 \times 9) = \square$

3. $14 \div (15 - 8) = \square$

4. $12 \div (18 \div 3) = \square$

5. $(22 - 8) \times 2 = \square$

6. $2 \times (10 + 5) = \square$

Solve these problems.

7. $6 + m = 9$
   $m = \square$

8. $t + 5 = 13$
   $t = \square$

9. $w - 1 = 7$
   $w = \square$

10. $6 - y = 2$
    $y = \square$

11. $20 - n = 11$
    $n = \square$

12. $25 - q = 19$
    $q = \square$

13. $r + 15 = 30$
    $r = \square$

14. $64 - s = 100$
    $s = \square$

 THINK $m \times 6$ has the same answer as $m \times 2 + 16$.
What is the value of m?

○ **I am confident with solving calculations using brackets
and finding a missing value in a problem.**

Solve these problems.

1 $(28 - 15) + 9 = \square$

2 $3 \times (117 - 95) = \square$

3 $2 \times (7{\cdot}2 \times 6) = \square$

4 $18 \div (3 \times 2) = \square$

5 $4 \times (9 \div 3) = \square$

6 $(6{\cdot}4 - 4{\cdot}2) \div 2 = \square$

Now find the value of the letter in each calculation.

7 $45 - d = 21$
$d = \square$

8 $78 - a = 45$
$a = \square$

9 $12 \times k = 96$
$k = \square$

10 $6h = 42$
$h = \square$

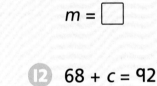

11 $\dfrac{88}{m} = 4$
$m = \square$

12 $68 + c = 92$
$c = \square$

13 $\dfrac{w}{3} = 12$
$w = \square$

14 $t - 36 = 54$
$t = \square$

 $m \times (6 + 3)$ has the same answer as $m \times 3 + 24$.
What is the value of m?

● ○ ○ **I am confident with solving calculations using brackets and finding a missing value in a problem.**

Solve these problems.

1. $(28 ÷ 7) + 93 =$ ☐

2. $275 - (160 + 17) =$ ☐

3. $(275 - 160) + 17 =$ ☐

4. $3 × (14 ÷ 7) + 5·5 =$ ☐

5. $9 ÷ (3 + 1·5) =$ ☐

6. $4 × (2·2 ÷ 2) - 3·4 =$ ☐

Now find the value of the letter in each calculation.

7. $m × 5 + 4 = 39$

   $m =$ ☐

8. $9 × (6 + j) = 81$

   $j =$ ☐

9. $t × 3 - 7 = 20$

   $t =$ ☐

10. $4 × (2 + s) = 48$

    $s =$ ☐

11. $2n + 3 = 21$

    $n =$ ☐

12. $w × (5 - 2) = 33$

    $w =$ ☐

13. $10 (q - 4) = 60$

    $q =$ ☐

14. $3 × (10 - y) = 27$

    $y =$ ☐

Using only these number cards, make the number sentence work.

$1\frac{1}{2}$ $2\frac{1}{2}$ $3\frac{1}{2}$ 2 3

15. $(☐ + ☐) × ☐ = 10$

$4 × (18 - m)$ has the same answer as $(16 - 12) × m$. What is the value of m?

○ **I am confident with solving calculations using brackets**
○ **and finding a missing value in a problem.**
○

Find the value of the letter in each calculation.

1. $5c + 4 = 54$
2. $4m + 5 = 17$
3. $10 - 2b = 4$
4. $20 - n = 3$
5. $3v + 4 = 12 - v$
6. $10 - b = 4b$

Find a pair of numbers that work in both equations.

7. $m + n + 2 = 11$
   $m - n = 5$
8. $p + q = 20$
   $2p = 10$
9. $a + 2b = 10$
   $a - b = 4$

Find the lengths of the missing sides.

10.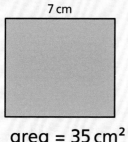

7 cm

area = 35 cm²

11.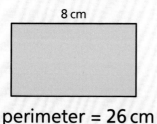

8 cm

perimeter = 26 cm

12.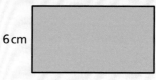

6 cm

area = 69 cm²

13.

5 cm

perimeter = 24 cm

Find the missing angles.

14.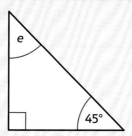

e

45°

15.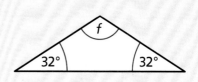

f

32°   32°

An isosceles triangle has one angle which is three times the value of the other two. What are its angles?

- I am confident with finding a missing value in a problem.

Find the value of the letter in each calculation.

1 $6c - 4 = 26$

2 $7r + 9 = 72$

3 $18 - 3b = 0$

4 $12 - n = 4 + n$

5 $6v - 3 = 32 - v$

6 $10 - 2q = 4q + 1$

Find a pair of numbers that work in both equations.

7 $m + 2n - 3 = 11$
$m + n = 9$

8 $2t + s = 9$
$t + 2s = 7.5$

9 $p + q = 10$
$3p - q = 2$

10 $w - 2y = 7$
$2w + y = 21.5$

11 $3a + b = 9$
$b - a = 5$

Find the lengths of the missing sides.

12
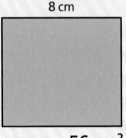
8 cm

area = 56 cm²

13
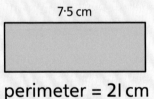
7·5 cm

perimeter = 21 cm

14
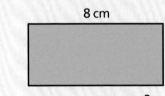
8 cm

area = 28 cm²

15
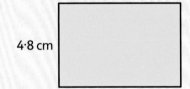
4·8 cm

perimeter = 28·8 cm

Find the missing angles.

16
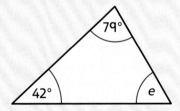
79°
42°
e

17
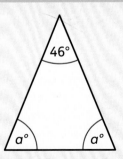
46°
a°
a°

● **I am confident with finding a missing value in a problem.**

Scaling by multiplying and dividing

Find the new dimensions.

1 A toy company has made a robot. They want to make a giant copy to help advertise their robot. The new robot will be 25 times bigger than the original. Work out the size of the new robot. Give your answers in metres.

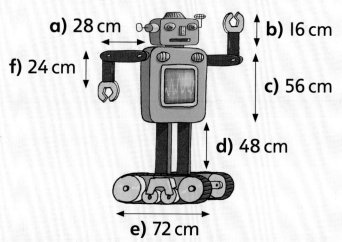

a) 28 cm **b)** 16 cm **f)** 24 cm **c)** 56 cm **d)** 48 cm **e)** 72 cm

2 The same toy company wants to make a toy dinosaur. They want to base it on a real dinosaur. The toy will be 20 times smaller than the real dinosaur. Work out the size of the toy. Give your answers in centimetres.

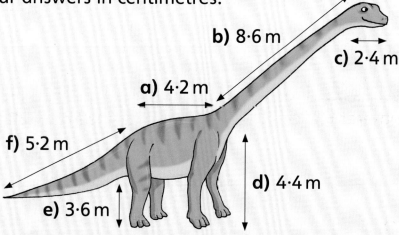

b) 8·6 m **c)** 2·4 m **a)** 4·2 m **f)** 5·2 m **d)** 4·4 m **e)** 3·6 m

THINK What would be a good way to multiply by 2·5? A good way to divide by 2·5? Try out your theory by solving 2·5 × 36 and 85 ÷ 2·5.

● I am confident with scaling up and down by multiplying
○ and dividing.
○

Answer the questions about the village.

1 The model village in Shearton is designed to be a perfect copy of the real village. Each feature has been made to be 25 times smaller. The map shows how tall some features are in the model village. Work out how tall each of these features is in real-life. Write your answer in metres.

a) 22·6 cm

b) 18 cm

c) 32·4 cm

d) 20·4 cm

e) 24·4 cm

f) 16·2 cm

Work out the size these models will be.

More features are going to be added. Each of these items will need to be made 25 times smaller to go in the model village. Write the new dimension for each model in centimetres.

2 A roundabout with a diameter of 3·6 m.

3 An office block that is 12·6 m wide.

4 Tennis courts that are 50·4 m across.

5 A memorial that is 4·8 m tall.

 THINK

The Eiffel tower is 320 m tall and its base is 104 m by 104 m. What would you need to divide each measurement by to make a model which would fit in the classroom but be big enough for small children to play in?

● **I am confident with scaling up and down by multiplying**
○ **and dividing.**
○
○

Multiplying by integers and decimals

Solve these multiplications.

1. 48 × 13 = ☐
2. 17 × 64 = ☐
3. £36 × 21 = ☐
4. 23 × 63 mm = ☐
5. 24 × 18 kg = ☐

6. 37 × 42 m = ☐
7. £45 × 54 = ☐
8. 38 × 42 l = ☐
9. £76 × 88 = ☐
10. 78 × 36 cm = ☐

Find the area of each playground.

11.
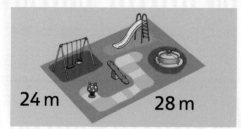
24 m   28 m

13.
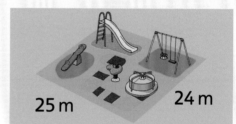
25 m   24 m

12.

13 m   22 m

14.
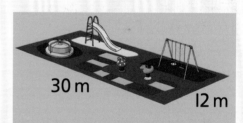
30 m   12 m

THINK

| 1 | 2 | 3 |

Put the number cards in the correct places to make this true.

☐ 4 × ☐ ☐ = 744

● I am confident with multiplying two 2-digit numbers.

29

Solve these multiplications.

1 632 × 4 = ☐

2 735 × 6 = ☐

3 375 × 3 = ☐

4 8134 × 5 = ☐

5 7056 × 8 = ☐

6 3972 × 9 = ☐

7 £7·39 × 8 = ☐

8 £9·78 × 4 = ☐

9 £79·45 × 9 = ☐

10 £18·57 × 6 = ☐

Now solve these word problems.

£3·48

£6·47

11 Sam's dad buys three P.E. t-shirts and three pairs of P.E. shorts. How much does he spend altogether?

12 Banu's mum buys four P.E. t-shirts and two pairs of P.E. shorts. How much does she spend altogether?

13 Mary's nan buys two P.E. t-shirts and four pairs of P.E. shorts. How much does she spend altogether?

14 Alex's mum buys four P.E. t-shirts and three pairs of P.E. shorts. How much does she spend altogether?

● I am confident with multiplying 4-digit numbers and
○ decimals by 1-digit numbers.
○

Find the perimeter of each of these regular shapes.

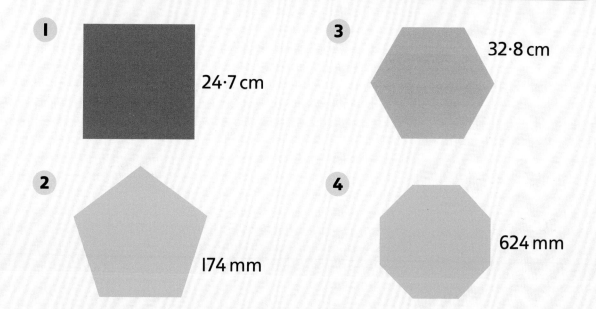

1. 24·7 cm

2. 174 mm

3. 32·8 cm

4. 624 mm

Now answer these word problems.

5. Clare buys four memory cards from an online store. Each card costs £23·74. There is also a £4·75 delivery charge. How much does she pay in total?

6. An adult ticket to a concert costs £58·67. A child's ticket is £13·24 cheaper than the adult ticket. How much would it cost for two adult and three children's tickets?

7. Sanjeet has just started a new job. He opens a bank account by paying in £50. Each month £68·72 in wages is paid into the account. How much will he have in the account after 6 months if he does not withdraw or spend any money?

8. Which is more expensive and by how much? Five pairs of trainers at £26·38 each or four pairs of boots at £31·89 each?

 Multiply 19·91 by 9. Then multiply 29·92 by 9. Then predict the answer to 39·93 × 9. Check your answer. Were you right?

● I am confident with multiplying 4-digit numbers and
○ decimals by 1-digit numbers.
○

31

Solve these multiplications.

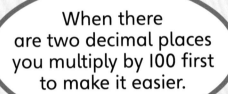

For questions with one decimal place you can multiply by 10 to get rid of the decimal point. Solve that multiplication and divide by 10 to answer the original question.

1 24 × 34·2 = ☐

24 × 342

	300	40	2
20	6000		
4			

So 24 × 34·2 = ☐

2 17 × 36·2 = ☐

3 22 × 123·4 = ☐

4 14 × 241·7 = ☐

5 26 × 2·42 = ☐

26 × 242 = ☐

So 26 × 2·42 = ☐

When there are two decimal places you multiply by 100 first to make it easier.

6 14 × 3·21 = ☐

7 24 × 2·79 = ☐

8 A slug crawls 23·2 cm in an hour. How far could it crawl in 24 hours?

9 Ibraheem cycles to and from his office every work day, which is a distance of 19·8 km. He works for 23 days in January. How far did he cycle on those days altogether?

10 Gary is 1·78 m tall. He can throw a javelin a distance that is 42 times his height. How far can he throw a javelin?

● I am confident with multiplying 4-digit numbers and
○ decimals by 2-digit numbers.
○
○

Write an estimation, then solve each problem.

1 $73{\cdot}2 \times 16 =$ ☐

5 $705{\cdot}6 \times 29 =$ ☐

2 $69{\cdot}5 \times 22 =$ ☐

6 $397{\cdot}2 \times 27 =$ ☐

3 $3{\cdot}77 \times 18 =$ ☐

7 $78{\cdot}69 \times 19 =$ ☐

4 $8{\cdot}34 \times 23 =$ ☐

8 $98{\cdot}78 \times 26 =$ ☐

9 Sara pays £5·89 each month in life insurance. How much does she pay in one year? How much does she pay in two years?

10 Pavlo is laying some square tiles, side-by-side in a row. Each tile is 38·4 cm long. How long is a row of 17 tiles?

11 What is the area of a field that is 132·4 m long by 28 m wide?

12 Chloe has a bank account that has £600 in it. Each month, for 18 months, she pays £28·57 from the account. How much money is left in the account after that, if no other money is paid in or withdrawn?

● I am confident with multiplying 4-digit numbers and
○ decimals by 2-digit numbers.

Solve these word problems.

1   Selina is getting car insurance for the year. If she pays up front she pays £444·11. How much more will she pay in total if she pays £37·46 each month for the year?

2   Along one side of a stretch of motorway, lamp-posts are spaced out so that each is 158·4 m from the next. There are 50 lamp-posts in a line. What is the distance from the first to the last lamp-post? (Clue: There are 49 spaces between them.)

3   A company makes rehydration sachets. Each sachet contains 19·45 g of medication. The company puts 24 sachets in each box. How much medication is in each box?

4   What is the area of a football pitch that measures 107·4 m long and 67 m wide?

5   Jack earns £47·52 each day. How much does he get paid for working 31 days?

6   The kerb stones along the edge of a road each measure 108·2 cm in length. What is the length of 27 kerb stones in a straight line?

7   Jasmine has a bank account that has £800 in it. Each month, for 16 months, she pays a direct debit of £46·77 from the account. How much money is left in the account after that, if no other money is paid in or withdrawn?

8   A large building is made using 84 steel girders, each measuring 14·35 m long. If each girder costs £23 per metre of its length, what is the total cost of the girders?

● I am confident with multiplying 4-digit numbers and
  decimals by 2-digit numbers.

Using division to find fractions of amounts

Solve these divisions.

1. a) $744 \div 6 = \square$

   b) $74 \cdot 4 \div 6 = \square$

   c) $7 \cdot 44 \div 6 = \square$

Your first answer in each group can help you solve the rest!

2. a) $528 \div 4 = \square$

   b) $52 \cdot 8 \div 4 = \square$

   c) $5 \cdot 28 \div 4 = \square$

3. a) $516 \div 3 = \square$

   b) $51 \cdot 6 \div 3 = \square$

   c) $5 \cdot 16 \div 3 = \square$

4. a) $963 \div 9 = \square$

   b) $96 \cdot 3 \div 9 = \square$

   c) $9 \cdot 63 \div 9 = \square$

5. a) $966 \div 7 = \square$

   b) $96 \cdot 6 \div 7 = \square$

   c) $9 \cdot 66 \div 7 = \square$

6. a) $1144 \div 8 = \square$

   b) $114 \cdot 4 \div 8 = \square$

   c) $11 \cdot 44 \div 8 = \square$

Now solve these word problems.

7. Nolberto needs to save £555 for a holiday in six months' time. If he saves the same amount each month for six months, how much must he save each month?

8. Mr Jones wins £253 and decides to give it to his four sons. How much do they each get if it is shared equally?

9. Eight children go on a week's holiday. They take a total of £580 in spending money. If each child takes the same amount, how much does each of them have?

THINK Choose the two questions you found trickiest and use multiplication to check your answers.

○ **I am confident with using division to find fractions of**
○ **amounts.**

35

How much does each child pay?

Different groups of children in Year 6 choose different end-of-term activities. Each group shares the cost of their activity equally. Work out how much each child will pay.

1

Total cost = £86·40

$\frac{1}{8}$ of £86·40 = ☐

3

Total cost = £76·80

2

Total cost = £48·00

4

Total cost = £102·20

Find the fractions of these decimal numbers.

5 $\frac{1}{5}$ of 181·5

6 $\frac{1}{4}$ of £210·40

7 $\frac{1}{8}$ of £356·80

8 $\frac{1}{6}$ of 828 kg

9 $\frac{1}{9}$ of 202·5 cm

10 $\frac{1}{6}$ of 319·2

11 $\frac{1}{5}$ of 131·5 m

12 $\frac{1}{3}$ of 861·6 km

13 $\frac{1}{7}$ of 882

14 $\frac{1}{8}$ of 623·2 l

> To help you answer the question, multiply by 10 or 100 to get rid of the decimal point. Then divide by 10 or 100 at the end.

THINK Is $\frac{1}{6}$ of 166 less than $\frac{1}{7}$ of 155? Estimate first then work out both to check your answer.

● ○ ○ **I am confident with using division to find fractions of amounts.**

How much does each child pay?

Different groups of children in Year 6 choose different end-of-term activities. Each group shares the cost of their activity equally. Work out how much each child will pay

1

Total cost = £202·50

$\frac{1}{9}$ of £202·50 = ☐

3

Total cost = £146·80

2

Total cost = £58·80

4

Total cost = £131·40

Now solve these word problems.

5 A group of four friends go out for dinner. The bill comes to £85·44. They decide to round it up to £100 as a tip. How much does each person pay towards the bill, and towards the tip?

6 Aswin needs to save £554 for a holiday in eight months' time. If he saves the same amount each month, how much must he save each month? If he saves £70 each month instead, how much extra will he save?

7 Mr Jones wins £537 in a competition. He spends £86 on himself and decides to give the rest to his four daughters. How much do they each get if it is shared equally?

 Is $\frac{1}{8}$ of 777 larger or smaller than $\frac{1}{9}$ of 888? Estimate first and then work out the divisions to check.

● **I am confident with using division to find fractions**
of amounts.

Dividing 4-digit numbers by 2-digit numbers

Write out the answers to the divisor's times table to help you.

Use long division to solve these problems.

$5836 \div 24 = \square$

$$
\begin{array}{r}
200 + 40 + 3, \text{ r4} \\
24\overline{\smash{\big)}\,5836} \\
-\ 4800 \\
\hline
1036 \\
-\ \ 960 \\
\hline
76 \\
-\ \ \ 72 \\
\hline
4
\end{array}
$$

24	144
48	168
72	192
96	216
120	240

1. $3699 \div 24 = \square$
2. $6742 \div 31 = \square$
3. $4678 \div 23 = \square$

4. $4578 \div 32 = \square$
5. $2465 \div 22 = \square$
6. $6487 \div 31 = \square$

7. $5876 \div 23 = \square$
8. $8764 \div 26 = \square$
9. $4445 \div 22 = \square$

10. Bottles in a factory are packed into crates that hold 24 bottles. How many crates are needed to hold 3699 bottles?

11. A company must supply at least 4658 flashcards to a distributor in 32 days' time. The machine that makes the flashcards is programmed to make the same whole number each day. How many should it be programmed for?

12. A shop buys jackets for £26. How many of them can they buy with £1745?

THINK If a whole number ending in 0 is divided by a 2-digit number ending in 2, the answer never has a remainder. Is this true? Try some divisions to find out.

I am confident with using long division to divide 4-digit numbers by 2-digit numbers.

Set out these problems and solve them using long division.

1. $2563 \div 33 = \square$ 6. $7253 \div 24 = \square$ 11. $4024 \div 27 = \square$

2. $5783 \div 27 = \square$ 7. $6234 \div 42 = \square$ 12. $7255 \div 24 = \square$

3. $5353 \div 34 = \square$ 8. $7426 \div 26 = \square$ 13. $6666 \div 34 = \square$

4. $6463 \div 42 = \square$ 9. $3068 \div 27 = \square$ 14. $2652 \div 27 = \square$

5. $2856 \div 33 = \square$ 10. $9321 \div 33 = \square$ 15. $9678 \div 42 = \square$

16. A company must supply at least 4024 batteries to a distributor in 27 days' time. The machine that makes the batteries is programmed to make the same whole number each day. How many should it be programmed for?

17. A craftsman wants to make 1646 wooden bowls over the next two years. How many bowls should he aim to make each month?

18. A shop buys mobile phones for £42. How many of them can they buy with £1745?

19. In a chocolate factory individual chocolates are put into boxes of 26. How many boxes can be filled with 3643 chocolates?

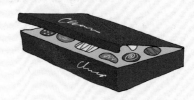

THINK   3001 is divided by an odd number and has a remainder of 5. What is the answer to the division?

Multiplication and division investigation

1   List the multiples of 16 from 1 × 16 through to 10 × 16.

2   Make up a 3-digit number where the last two digits are a multiple of 4, for example 764 or 328.

3   Divide this number by 16. Find the exact answer, writing the fraction part of the answer as a decimal where you can.

$$764 \div 16 = 47\frac{12}{16} = 47\frac{3}{4} = 47 \cdot 75$$

4   Repeat for other 3-digit numbers and then for some 4-digit numbers. The last two digits must be a multiple of 4.

5   What do you notice?

6   Now try this with numbers where the last two digits are not a multiple of 4. What happens now?

● **I am confident with multiplying and dividing by 16.**
○
○

Dividing with a decimal remainder

Find the exact answers to these divisions. Write fractions as decimals where you can.

$$426 \div 12 = 35\frac{6}{12} = 35\frac{1}{2} = 35{\cdot}5$$

1. $426 \div 12 = \boxed{}$
2. $867 \div 24 = \boxed{}$
3. $729 \div 12 = \boxed{}$
4. $531 \div 24 = \boxed{}$
5. $426 \div 24 = \boxed{}$

6. $531 \div 15 = \boxed{}$
7. $426 \div 15 = \boxed{}$
8. $867 \div 12 = \boxed{}$
9. $729 \div 24 = \boxed{}$
10. $531 \div 12 = \boxed{}$

11. $729 \div 18 = \boxed{}$
12. $531 \div 18 = \boxed{}$
13. $426 \div 18 = \boxed{}$
14. $867 \div 15 = \boxed{}$
15. $729 \div 15 = \boxed{}$

Solve these word problems.

16. Twenty-four friends went out for a meal. The total bill came to £654. If they choose to split the bill equally, how much should they each pay?

17. Over an 18-month period, Jack was given £459 in pocket money. How much was this per month?

18. A farmer's field has a wall that is 366 m long. The farmer wants to put a fence beside the wall to stop his sheep jumping over the wall. He wants to split the length into 15 equal sections. How wide should each section be?

 THINK Some people are going to a pizza party. There are 16 of them and they share the cost. The bill comes to £212. How much do they each pay?

- I am confident with changing fraction remainders into decimals.

Coordinates

Work out the missing coordinates.

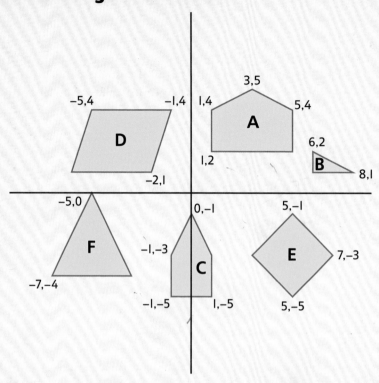

1. A is a symmetrical pentagon. Write the coordinates of the missing vertex.

2. B is a right-angled triangle. Write the coordinates of the missing vertex.

3. C is a symmetrical pentagon. Write the coordinates of the missing vertex.

4. D is a parallelogram. Write the coordinates of the missing vertex.

5. E is a square. Write the coordinates of the missing vertex.

6. F is an isosceles triangle. Write the coordinates of the missing vertex.

 Make up your own coordinates for the points of a square.

Adding and subtracting fractions

$$\frac{3}{4} + \frac{2}{3} = \square$$

$$= \frac{9}{12} + \frac{8}{12}$$

$$= \frac{17}{12}$$

$$= 1\frac{5}{12}$$

Write both as $\frac{1}{12}$ s.

1. $\frac{2}{5} + 4 = \square$

2. $\frac{2}{3} + \frac{5}{6} = \square$

3. $\frac{2}{5} + \frac{2}{3} = \square$

4. $\frac{3}{4} + \frac{1}{5} = \square$

5. $\frac{2}{3} + \frac{2}{4} = \square$

6. $\frac{7}{8} - \frac{2}{3} = \square$

7. $\frac{2}{5} - \frac{1}{6} = \square$

8. $1\frac{2}{9} - \frac{2}{3} = \square$

9. $1\frac{4}{5} - \frac{3}{4} = \square$

10. $\frac{8}{9} - \frac{1}{5} = \square$

Write both fractions out with the same denominator.

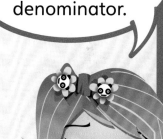

THINK How can you use what you have just practised to work out $\frac{2}{5} + 0.8$? What is the answer?

● I am confident with adding and subtracting fractions.
○
○
○

Multiplying and dividing with fractions

Solve these multiplications.

1 $5 \times \frac{1}{4} = \square$

5 $8 \times \frac{1}{5} = \square$

2 $7 \times \frac{1}{6} = \square$

6 $10 \times \frac{1}{7} = \square$

3 $11 \times \frac{1}{3} = \square$

7 $15 \times \frac{1}{4} = \square$

4 $8 \times \frac{1}{4} = \square$

8 $50 \times \frac{1}{9} = \square$

Answer these divisions.

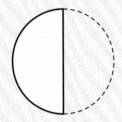 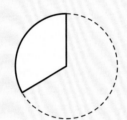 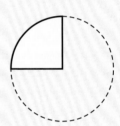

9 $\frac{1}{2} \div 2 = \square$

12 $\frac{1}{3} \div 2 = \square$

15 $\frac{1}{4} \div 2 = \square$

10 $\frac{1}{2} \div 3 = \square$

13 $\frac{1}{3} \div 3 = \square$

16 $\frac{1}{4} \div 3 = \square$

11 $\frac{1}{2} \div 4 = \square$

14 $\frac{1}{3} \div 4 = \square$

17 $\frac{1}{4} \div 4 = \square$

Write a multiplication where the answer is smaller than both of the numbers being multiplied. Write one where the answer is bigger than both numbers being multiplied.

I am confident with multiplying and dividing fractions.

Answer these multiplications and divisions.

1. $12 \times \frac{1}{6} = \square$

2. $\frac{1}{6} \div 2 = \square$

3. $11 \times \frac{1}{2} = \square$

4. $\frac{1}{6} \div 3 = \square$

5. $22 \times \frac{1}{4} = \square$

6. $24 \times \frac{1}{5} = \square$

7. $\frac{1}{8} \div 3 = \square$

8. $15 \times \frac{1}{8} = \square$

9. $\frac{1}{3} \div 4 = \square$

10. $\frac{1}{3} \div 3 = \square$

Now solve these questions.

11.

$\frac{1}{2}$ of $\frac{2}{3}$

$\frac{1}{4}$ of $\frac{2}{3}$

12.

$\frac{1}{2} \times \frac{3}{4}$

$\frac{1}{3} \times \frac{3}{4}$

Multiply these fractions together.

13. $\frac{1}{3} \times \frac{2}{3} = \square$

14. $\frac{1}{4} \times \frac{1}{3} = \square$

15. $\frac{1}{3} \times \frac{4}{9} = \square$

16. $\frac{1}{4} \times \frac{3}{4} = \square$

17. $\frac{1}{5} \times \frac{3}{4} = \square$

18. $\frac{1}{3} \times \frac{4}{5} = \square$

19. $\frac{1}{2} \times \frac{3}{8} = \square$

20. $\frac{1}{3} \times \frac{7}{8} = \square$

21. $\frac{1}{7} \times \frac{2}{3} = \square$

 What number can multiply a number of thirds, quarters and sixths to give a whole number answer? Test out your suggestion.

● I am confident with multiplying and dividing fractions.
○
○

Answer these multiplications and divisions.

1. $14 \times \frac{1}{6} = \square$

2. $\frac{1}{5} \div 7 = \square$

3. $11 \times \frac{1}{7} = \square$

4. $\frac{1}{6} \div 6 = \square$

5. $30 \times \frac{1}{4} = \square$

6. $67 \times \frac{1}{9} = \square$

7. $\frac{1}{8} \div 7 = \square$

8. $42 \times \frac{1}{8} = \square$

9. $\frac{1}{9} \div 5 = \square$

10. $\frac{1}{7} \div 3 = \square$

Multiply these pairs of fractions.

11. $\frac{1}{4} \times \frac{3}{5} = \square$

12. $\frac{4}{5} \times \frac{2}{3} = \square$

13. $\frac{2}{7} \times \frac{2}{3} = \square$

14. $\frac{2}{3} \times \frac{5}{6} = \square$

15. $\frac{3}{5} \times \frac{4}{5} = \square$

16. $\frac{2}{9} \times \frac{3}{4} = \square$

17. $\frac{3}{5} \times \frac{6}{7} = \square$

18. $\frac{2}{3} \times \frac{7}{8} = \square$

19. $\frac{5}{7} \times \frac{2}{3} = \square$

THINK

What is $\frac{1}{2}$ squared? What is $\frac{1}{3}$ squared? What is $\frac{1}{4}$ squared? What is $\frac{1}{5}$ squared? Is the square of a fraction that is less than 1 larger or smaller than the fraction itself?

● I am confident with multiplying and dividing fractions.
○
○

Ratio

Solve the word problems.

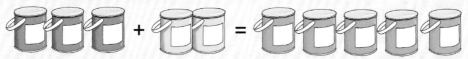

1. How many tins of yellow paint are needed to make 10 tins of green paint?

2. How many tins of blue paint are needed to make 25 tins of green paint?

3. You have lots of tins of yellow paint but only 9 tins of blue paint. How many tins of green paint can you make?

 300 g    200 g   100 g

4. These are the ingredients for six pieces of shortbread. How much of the ingredients would be needed to make 12 pieces of shortbread?

5. How much of the ingredients would be needed to make 9 pieces?

6. Sarah uses 900 g of flour. How much butter and sugar should she use?

7. Poor Cat tried to make 15 pieces of shortbread. She used 800 g of flour, 600 g of butter and 250 g of sugar. How much should she have used?

8.  A smoothie is made with 10 strawberries, 15 raspberries and 100 ml of apple juice. If Jarek uses 20 strawberries, how much of the other ingredients does he need?

 THINK Some purple paint has a ratio of 4 parts blue to 7 parts red. If Dad decides it is too bluish, what ratio can he try? How much red would he then need if he uses 300 ml of blue?

○ **I am confident with solving word problems involving ratio.**

Solve these ratio problems.

60p per 100g

1. How much would 1 kg of cherries cost?

2. Francis spends £3 on cherries. What weight of cherries did he buy?

3. Jess spends £1·80 on cherries. What weight did she buy?

£8·40 for 1 kg

4. Marek buys 1 kg of cheese. How much does this cost?

5. Ibraheem's dad buys 500 g of cheese. How much does this cost?

6. Ibraheem has to go to the shops to buy an extra 250 g of cheese. How much money does his dad have to give him?

RECIPE
600 g oats
240 g butter
makes
8 slices

7. This recipe for flapjacks uses 600 g of oats and 240 g of butter to make 8 slices. How much butter should Jane use to make 4 slices?

8. Kim has only 450 g of oats. How much butter should she use and how many slices will she make?

9. A school cook wants to make 20 slices of flapjack. How much oats and butter does she need?

THINK In a sponge cake the ratio of flour to sugar to fat is 3 to 2 to 1. If Mary's gran makes a cake with 150 g of sugar, how much flour and fat will she use?

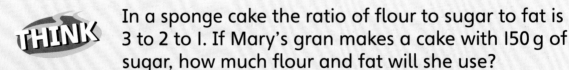

● I am confident with solving word problems involving ratio.
○
○
○

Reading scales and measures problems

Write the value for each scale.

1

4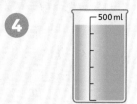

7

2

5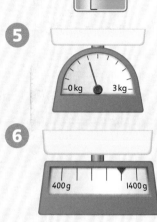

8

3

6

9

Now solve these problems.

10

a) If 150 ml is added, how much will be in the jar?

b) If 300 ml is taken out, how much will be left in the jar?

Can you solve this challenge?

11 Devise a noise scale to monitor the amount of noise in the classroom. The 'noise units' are decibels. We know that:

Near silence is 0 decibels
A whisper is 15 decibels
Normal adult talk is 50 decibels
A lawnmower is 90 decibels
A rock concert or jet engine is 120 decibels.

Draw your classroom noise scale, then mark the noise levels at the end of the day and at a quiet reading time. Can you mark some other times as well?

○ **I am confident with reading and creating scales.**
○
○

1. Hassan adds another 140 ml to his jug. How much water is in the jug now?

2. Hassan now pours 200 ml away. How much water is left?

3. What is the total length of all three items? Give your answer in mm.

4. What is the length of the key in mm?

5. Both of these containers are emptied into a bucket. How much liquid is there in the bucket?

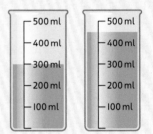

6. How much do these apples weigh altogether?

7. How much more would you have to buy if you wanted 1 kg of apples?

8. Maddie eats the largest apple on the scale. It weighs 200 g. What weight of apples is left?

9. How much water would you have to pour out of the first container if you wanted it to contain the same amount of water as the second container?

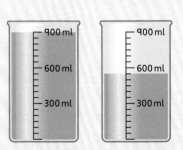

10. How much water is in both containers combined?

I am confident with solving problems involving measures.

Properties of 2D shapes

Work out the missing angles.

1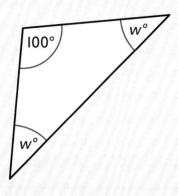

100° w°

w°

3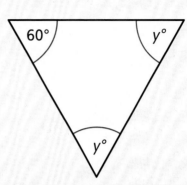

60° y°

y°

2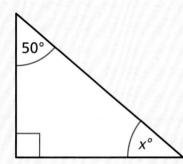

50°

x°

4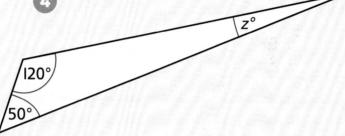

z°

120°

50°

Find the area of each shape.

5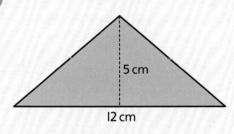

5 cm

12 cm

area = ☐ cm²

6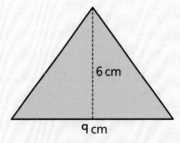

6 cm

9 cm

area = ☐ cm²

THINK In a right-angled triangle, the longest side is always opposite the right angle. Is this statement always true? Explain why.

● I am confident with calculating the properties of shapes.
○
○

Write the missing angles for each shape.

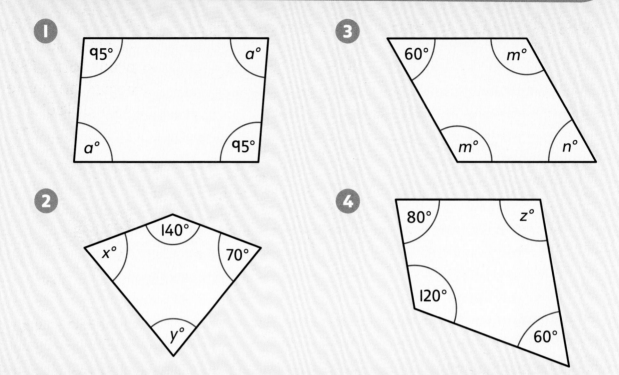

1. 95°, a°, a°, 95°

3. 60°, m°, m°, n°

2. 140°, x°, 70°, y°

4. 80°, z°, 120°, 60°

Find the perimeter and area of each shape.

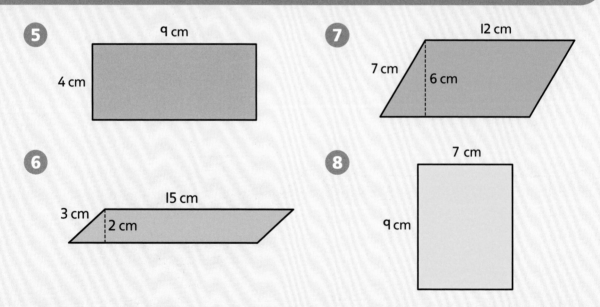

5. 9 cm, 4 cm

7. 12 cm, 7 cm, 6 cm

6. 15 cm, 3 cm, 2 cm

8. 7 cm, 9 cm

THINK Using a pair of scissors and a drawing of a quadrilateral, how can you demonstrate that the four angles in any quadrilateral add to 360°?

● **I am confident with calculating the properties of shapes.**
○
○

Measuring and calculating angles

Write the missing angles for each question.

Angles around a point total 360°. Angles on a line total 180°.

1 105° a°

2 x° 50°

3 m° n° 60° 120°

4 30° a°

5 x°

6 a°

7 t°

8 m°

9 35° 45° x°

10 25° y° 95°

 **THINK** There are three angles round a point. One is a right angle and the second is twice the size of the third. What are the angles?

● ○ ○ **I am confident with calculating the properties of shapes.**

Find the missing angles in each question.

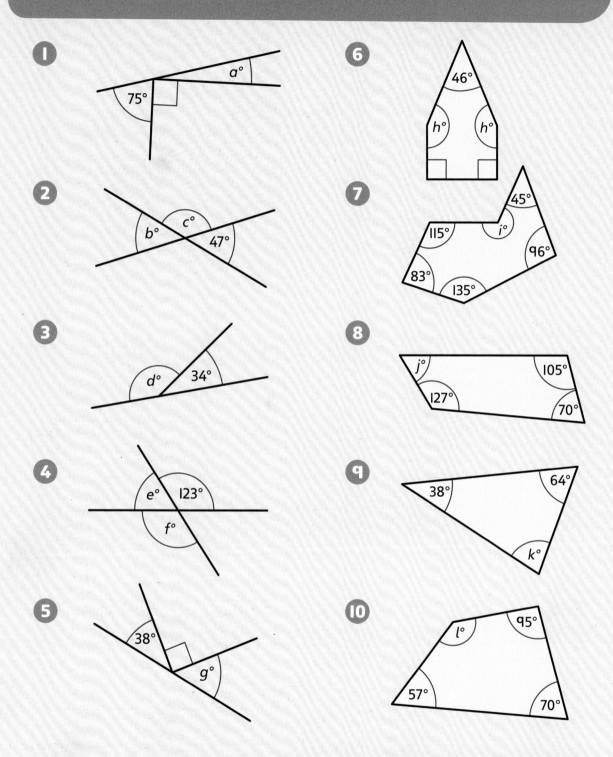

1
a°
75°

2
b°   c°
47°

3
d°   34°

4
e°   123°
f°

5
38°
g°

6
46°
h°   h°

7
45°
115°   i°
96°
83°
135°

8
j°
105°
127°
70°

9
38°
64°
k°

10
l°   95°
57°
70°

THINK There are three angles on a straight line. The first one is twice the size of the second. The third one is three times the size of the second. What are the angles?

○ **I am confident with calculating missing angles.**

Work out the missing angles in each shape.

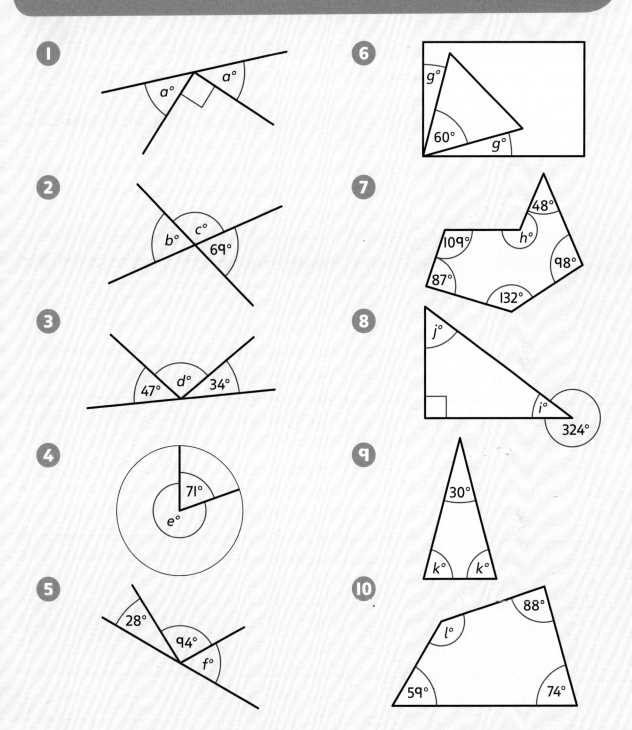

1

a° *a°*

2

b° *c°*
69°

3

47° *d°* 34°

4

71°
e°

5

28°
94°
f°

6

g°
60°
g°

7

48°
109° *h°*
98°
87°
132°

8

j°
i°
324°

9

30°
k° *k°*

10

88°
l°
59° 74°

THINK There are four angles around a point. The first one is twice the size of the second. The third one is three times the size of the second. The fourth one is four times the size of the second. What are the angles?

I am confident with calculating missing angles.

Area, perimeter and volume

Find the area and perimeter of each shape.

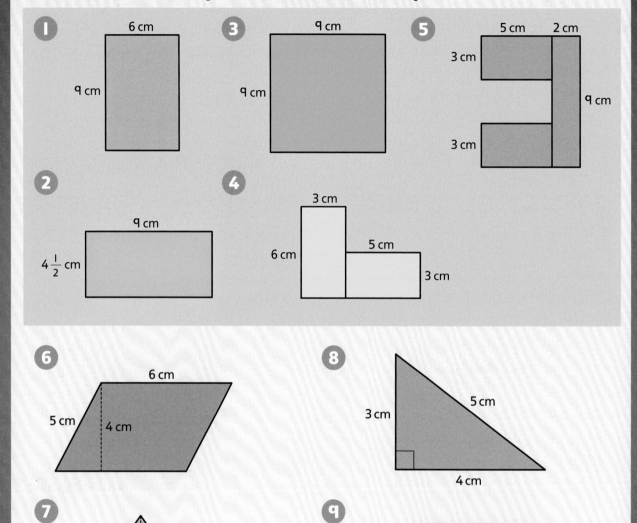

1 6 cm, 9 cm

3 9 cm, 9 cm

5 5 cm, 2 cm, 3 cm, 9 cm, 3 cm

2 9 cm, $4\frac{1}{2}$ cm

4 3 cm, 6 cm, 5 cm, 3 cm

6 6 cm, 5 cm, 4 cm

8 3 cm, 5 cm, 4 cm

7 5 cm, 5 cm, 4 cm, 6 cm

9 7·5 cm, 6 cm, 8 cm

A parallelogram has a height half the size of the length of its longer side. Its area is 32 cm². Draw a parallelogram like this and calculate its perimeter.

○ **I am confident with calculating the area and perimeter**
○ **of 2D shapes.**

Find the areas and perimeters of these shapes.

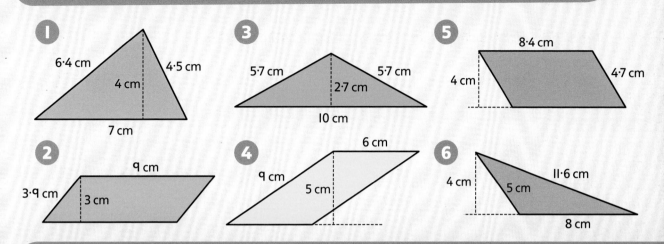

1 6·4 cm 4·5 cm 4 cm 7 cm

2 9 cm 3·9 cm 3 cm

3 5·7 cm 5·7 cm 2·7 cm 10 cm

4 6 cm 9 cm 5 cm

5 8·4 cm 4 cm 4·7 cm

6 4 cm 5 cm 11·6 cm 8 cm

Find the volume of each of these cuboids.

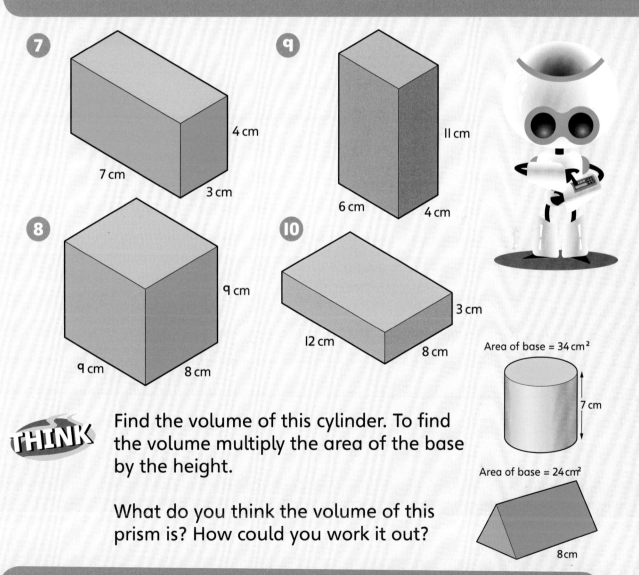

7 4 cm 7 cm 3 cm

8 9 cm 9 cm 8 cm

9 11 cm 6 cm 4 cm

10 3 cm 12 cm 8 cm

THINK Find the volume of this cylinder. To find the volume multiply the area of the base by the height.

Area of base = 34 cm² 7 cm

What do you think the volume of this prism is? How could you work it out?

Area of base = 24 cm² 8 cm

I am confident with calculating the area and perimeter of 2D shapes and the volume of 3D shapes.

57

intervals of time

Answer these questions about time.

1.  Look at this clock. Write the time shown as a digital time.

2. Write 4:45 pm as a 24-hour digital time.

3.  Look at this clock. What was the time an hour earlier?

4.  Look at this clock. What is the time going to be 25 minutes later?

Use the timetable to answer these questions.

Shubunkin pool activity times		
	Begins	**Ends**
Family swim	2:05 pm	3:15 pm
Wet and wild	3:15 pm	5:10 pm
Water slides	5:10 pm	6:30 pm
Free swim	6:30 pm	9:00 pm

5. Jo arrives at the pool at quarter to five in the afternoon. How long does she have to wait until Water slides starts?

6. How much longer is the length of time for Free swim than the length of time for Family swim?

 THINK How many hour and a half long DVDs could you watch if you got home from school at half past four and went to bed at nine o'clock?

I am confident with answering questions involving intervals of time.

Answer these time questions.

1  Look at this clock. What time would it be 25 minutes earlier? Write your answer as a 12-hour digital time.

2  Look at this clock. Write the time it shows as a 24-hour digital time.

3 Pedal boat hire costs £5 for an hour or £10 for three hours. How much does it cost to hire a boat for 6 hours? How much would it cost to hire a boat for 4 hours?

Look at this bus timetable. Use the information to answer the questions below.

Sutton	07:35		11:45	14:15	17:15
Erdington	07:55	08:20		14:35	17:35
Handsworth	08:20	08:45	12:30		18:00
Aston		09:05	12:50	15:20	18:20
Longbridge	09:20	09:45	13:30	16:00	

4 How long is there between the first two buses to leave Sutton?

5 Parveen needs to be in Longbridge by 2 pm. What is the latest bus she can take from Sutton to reach there in time?

6 Sam gets on the bus in Erdington at twenty-five to three. The bus is on time and he gets off at the next stop. Where does he get off and at what time? Give the time in 12-hour digital time, using am or pm.

 A cake has to be baked for 35 minutes and needs to be ready for ten past four. If it needs to cool for half an hour, what time is the latest time it can be put in the oven?

○ **I am confident with answering questions involving**
○ **intervals of time.**
○

This timetable shows the times trains stop at different stations. Use the information to answer the questions below.

London	06:55	08:30	09:25		16:48
Birmingham	09:10	10:34	11:31	14:11	18:55
Leeds	11:07	12:29		15:18	20:44
Newcastle	12:45	14:05		17:10	22:23
Edinburgh	13:55		16:00	18:28	23:39
Aberdeen	15:15	16:30	17:15	19:57	

1 Kylie gets to Birmingham station at 10:40 and catches the next train to Aberdeen. If she had arrived 10 minutes earlier at Birmingham station, how much earlier could she have arrived in Aberdeen?

2 Tom caught the train in London at five to seven and got off in Leeds to visit a friend. He spent 3 hours with his friend and then got on the next train from Leeds to Aberdeen. What time did he arrive in Aberdeen? Write the time in words.

Now answer these other word problems.

3 Andrea leaves Bristol at 13:23. Her journey takes 2 hours and 50 minutes. When does she arrive? Write the time in words.

4 Lorenzo arrives in Compton at 23:01. If his journey took 12 hours and 15 minutes, what time did he leave? Write the time in 24-hour digital time.

Perth in Western Australia is 8 hours ahead of the UK. Sunil lives in Perth and wants to talk to his friend Katie. Katie lives in London. They both work from 9 am to 5 pm each day. Between what times in Perth could Sunil phone Katie when neither of them is working?

I am confident with answering questions involving intervals of time.

Interpreting graphs

Answer the questions about each graph.

This pictogram shows the number of hits on different charities' websites over the course of a day.

Charity A	⊕ ⊕ ⊕ ⊕ ⊕ ⊕
Charity B	⊕ ⊕ ◂
Charity C	⊕ ⊕ ⊕ ◖
Charity D	⊕ ⊕ ⊕ ⊕ ⊕ ◂

⊕ = 100 hits

1 How many hits did Charity D's website receive?

2 If Charity C has a target of 500 hits a day, how many more does it need to reach this total?

3 How many more hits did Charity A receive than Charity B?

4 What was the total number of hits received by all four charities?

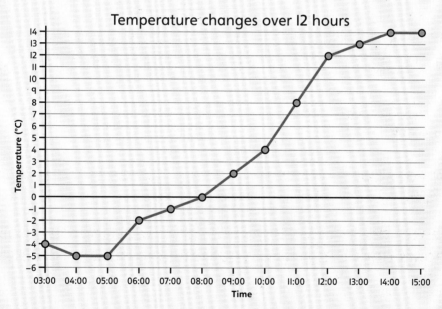

Temperature changes over 12 hours

5 What was the temperature at 6 o'clock in the morning?

6 How much warmer was it at midday than at 3 am?

7 At what time would you estimate the temperature was 3 °C?

8 What would you estimate the temperature might have been at 8:30 and at 11:30?

Year 6 voted on who would win the league. Answer the questions about the results.

1. How many more children voted for Didcot Athletic than Headingly Palace?

2. How many teams received more than 13 votes? Which teams were they?

3. Some Year 5 children also voted. If 17 of them voted for Newtown Rovers, how many more was this than the number of Year 6 who voted for Newtown Rovers?

4. How many Year 6 children voted altogether?

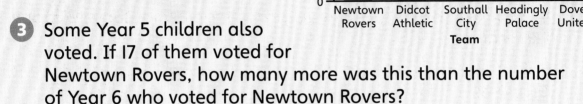

This line graph shows how high a man climbed during a day.

5. By what time had the man climbed up 1500 m?

6. Approximately how high had he climbed by three o'clock in the afternoon?

7. About how high had the man climbed before he stopped for an hour's break?

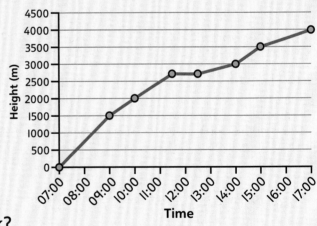

8. How much further did he climb in the three hours between 7 am and 10 am than in the three hours between 2 pm and 5 pm. Why do you think this was?

○ **I am confident with reading and interpreting graphs.**

These pie charts show how children would like to spend their time. There are 80 children in Year 6 and only 60 in Year 2.

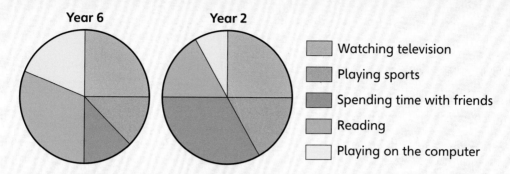

Year 6   Year 2

☐ Watching television
☐ Playing sports
☐ Spending time with friends
☐ Reading
☐ Playing on the computer

1 In Year 6, if 15 children like playing on the computer how many like reading?

2 Is it true to say the same number of children like to watch TV in Year 2 as in Year 6? Explain your answer.

3 Is it true to say the same number of children like to play sports in Year 2 as in Year 6? Explain your answer.

4 How many more children in Year 6 like to read than in Year 2?

Use the conversion chart to answer the questions.

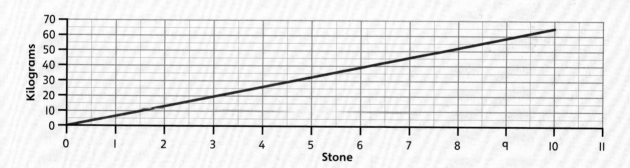

Approximately how many kilograms are equivalent to:

5 3 stone?   6 $7\frac{1}{2}$ stone?   7 85 stone?

About how many stone is equivalent to:

8 10 kg?   9 40 kg?   10 250 kg?

I am confident with reading and interpreting graphs.

Money investigation

Swindling Syd offers you a job for 50 days.

You can either be paid:

Ip on day I		£100 on day I
2p on day 2	**OR**	£200 on day 2
4p on day 3		£300 on day 3
8p on day 4		£400 on day 4
(Double the previous day)		(Add £100 each day)

1. Which do you think is better?

2. How much would you be paid on the 20th day using each system?

3. Would you change your mind now?

4. Which is the better deal?

5. Can you work out how much you would be paid in total for the second option?

I am confident with solving problems involving large numbers.

Unusual multiplication methods

Practise Brahmagupta's multiplication method.

351 × 628 = 220 428

```
3    6  2  8              3    6  2  8
5       6  2  8           5       6  2  8
1          6  2  8        1          6  2  8
───────────────          ──────────────────
                         1  8  8  4
        ──→               3  1  4  0
                                6  2  8
                         1  1  1
                         2  2  0  4  2  8
```

> Line up the hundreds digit in each answer row with the hundreds digit in its question.

Now solve these multiplications using Brahmagupta's method.

1 67 × 242 = ☐

2 34 × 427 = ☐

3 18 × 354 = ☐

4 52 × 287 = ☐

5 324 × 267 = ☐

6 421 × 352 = ☐

7 624 × 145 = ☐

8 178 × 524 = ☐

- I am confident with solving multiplication problems using Brahmagupta's method.

0	1	2	3	4	5	6	7	8	9
0/0	0/2	0/4	0/6	0/8	1/0	1/2	1/4	1/6	1/8
0/0	0/3	0/6	0/9	1/2	1/5	1/8	2/1	2/4	2/7
0/0	0/4	0/8	1/2	1/6	2/0	2/4	2/8	3/2	3/6
0/0	0/5	1/0	1/5	2/0	2/5	3/0	3/5	4/0	4/5
0/0	0/6	1/2	1/8	2/4	3/0	3/6	4/2	4/8	5/4
0/0	0/7	1/4	2/1	2/8	3/5	4/2	4/9	5/6	6/3
0/0	0/8	1/6	2/4	3/2	4/0	4/8	5/6	6/4	7/2
0/0	0/9	1/8	2/7	3/6	4/5	5/4	6/3	7/2	8/1

Use Napier's bones to work out these multiplications.

1 3245 × 6 = ☐

2 1784 × 5 = ☐

3 4732 × 8 = ☐

4 67 213 × 4 = ☐

5 52 431 × 6 = ☐

6 31 178 × 7 = ☐

7 3457 × 32 = ☐

8 4215 × 24 = ☐

9 2721 × 17 = ☐

10 32 143 × 24 = ☐

11 18 256 × 32 = ☐

12 24 142 × 43 = ☐

13 Use the grid method to check two of your calculations. Do the same numbers appear in both methods?

Try 1234 × 9, then 12345 × 9 and 123 456 × 9 using Napier's bones. Then predict the answer to 1234 567 × 9.

● **I am confident with solving multiplication problems using Napier's bones.**

Use the lattice method to help you solve multiplication questions.

42 × 57 = 2394

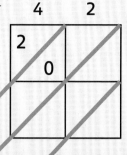
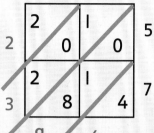

4 × 5 = 20

Solve these questions using the lattice method.

1. 14 × 23 = ☐
2. 22 × 46 = ☐
3. 34 × 27 = ☐
4. 26 × 34 = ☐
5. 51 × 36 = ☐

6. 43 × 55 = ☐
7. 37 × 58 = ☐
8. 18 × 74 = ☐
9. 66 × 47 = ☐
10. 89 × 68 = ☐

What will you do if the numbers in a lattice row add to more than 9?

Answer these word problems.

11. James saved 28p each day for the 31 days of January. How much did he save?

12. How many hours are there in 43 days?

 Choose the two questions you found trickiest to solve. Check your answers using the grid method. Which method do you find easier? Why?

● I am confident with solving multiplication problems
○ using the lattice method.

Solve these problems using the lattice method.

58 × 254 = 14 732

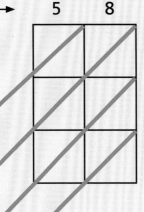 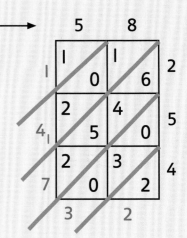

1 26 × 473 = ☐

2 63 × 271 = ☐

3 335 × 68 = ☐

4 41 × 317 = ☐

5 242 × 39 = ☐

6 42 × 653 = ☐

7 534 × 82 = ☐

8 924 × 75 = ☐

9 36 × 174 = ☐

10 539 × 68 = ☐

Answer these word problems.

11 How many hours are there in 365 days?

12 A factory makes biscuits that are put into packets of 26.
If it makes biscuits for 372 packets, how many fewer than
10 000 biscuits does it make?

 Write a multiplication which is easier to solve using the
grid method. Write one which is easy to solve using a
different written method. Write one which is easy to solve
mentally. What makes a multiplication easy to solve?

● I am confident with solving multiplication problems
using the lattice method.

Use the grid method, Brahmagupta's method, Napier's bones and the lattice method to work out each of these multiplications.

1 24 × 326 = ☐   **3** 4278 × 14 = ☐

Make sure you try all four methods for each problem!

2 43 × 627 = ☐   **4** 6214 × 28 = ☐

5 Which is your favourite method?

6 Which do you think is the quickest?

7 Which is the easiest to understand?

8 Which is your least favourite method and why?

9 If you were a Year 6 teacher, which method would you teach? Why?

○ **I am confident with solving multiplication problems**
○ **using different written methods.**

Binary numbers

Write these binary numbers using the decimal system.

	16s	8s	4s	2s	Is
1			I	I	I
2		I	0	I	0
3	I	0	I	I	0
4	I	I	0	0	I

 Look at questions 5–10. Can you predict which binary numbers will be odd?

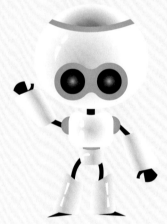

5 I0I

6 II00

7 II0I0

8 I0I0I

9 IIIII

10 I0000I

Copy and complete these sentences. Use binary numbers to complete them.

11 A spider has ☐ legs.

12 A table has ☐ legs.

13 There are ☐ months in a year.

14 I am ☐ years old.

● **I am confident with reading and writing binary numbers.**
○
○

Magic Squares

Copy these squares. Write numbers in the spaces so that each side in a square has the same total.

1

6	3	3
5	■	
	5	6

2

1	3	6
7	■	
	8	

3

8	4	
2	■	10
5		2

4

		1
	■	
5	0	8

5 Now make up four of your own squares. For each square choose a different side total from the box.

10	14	16	20	22	24

I am confident with solving number problems.

Solve these magic squares. Each horizontal, vertical and diagonal must add to 15. Each number 1–9 can only be used once in a square.

1

4	3	
	5	1
2		

3

		6
9	5	
	3	

2

		2
	5	
	1	

4

8		6
	5	

5 Now create your own magic squares. Each row, column and diagonal must add to 15.

The number 5 always goes in the middle.

I am confident with solving number problems.

Mystery tables

The times tables on this page have been written in code. Can you crack the code?

The letters A–J stand for each of the digits 0–9. The code is not in order, so A is not I. You will have to work out which letter is which digit.

Copy and complete each table. Copy and complete the key. The key is the same for each table and will help you solve the rest.

1 E × F = F
2 A × F = EB
3 C × F = AH
4 G × F = CI

5 D × F = GD
6 I × F = DG
7 H × F = IC
8 B × F = HA

9 F × F = BE
10 EJ × F = FJ
11 EE × F = FF
12 EA × F = EJB

13 A = ☐
14 B = ☐
15 C = ☐
16 D = ☐
17 E = ☐
18 F = ☐
19 G = ☐
20 H = ☐
21 I = ☐
22 J = ☐

23 I × A = EA
24 A × A = G
25 C × A = I
26 EJ × A = AJ

27 H × A = EG
28 EE × A = AA
29 D × A = EJ
30 B × A = EI

31 F × A = AB
32 G × A = B
33 E × A = A
34 EA × A = AG

35 I × C = EB
36 A × C = I
37 D × C = ED
38 B × C = AG

39 C × C = F
40 EJ × C = CJ
41 H × C = AE
42 G × C = EA

43 EE × C = CC
44 E × C = C
45 F × C = AH
46 EA × C = CI

47 I × I = CI
48 A × I = EA
49 C × I = EB
50 D × I = CJ

51 G × I = AG
52 E × I = I
53 EJ × I = IJ
54 B × I = GB

55 F × I = DG
56 H × I = GA
57 EA × I = HA
58 EE × I = II

THINK Use the same code to write the 5 times table and then your own choice of times table. Can your partner work out which table it is?

● I am confident with solving missing number problems.
○
○

The Fibonacci Sequence

This is the Fibonacci sequence:

1	1	2	3	5	8	13

Use the same rule to write the next three numbers in these sequences.

1. 5, 6, 11, 17, 28, 45, …

2. 3, 4, 7, 11, 18, 29, …

3. 2, 4, 6, 10, 16, 26, …

4. 5, 7, 12, 19, 31, 50, …

5. –1, 1, 0, 1, 1, 2, …

This is a sequence of triangular numbers.

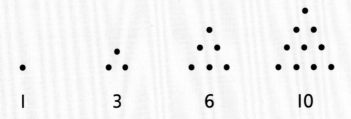

1   3   6   10

6. Write the next six numbers.
7. Write a rule for finding the next number.

● I am confident with using a rule to find the next
  numbers in a sequence.

1 This chart shows the cost of printing photos and postage.

Standard size	12p per print
Enlarged size	27p per print
Postage	£2·10 per order

Jade orders **7 standard sized prints** and **5 enlarged prints**.
What is the total cost, including postage?

2 In a school talent show Dean gets 76 votes.
Sandeep gets exactly **four times as many** votes as Dean.

How many votes does Sandeep get?

3 In a box there are **3 milk chocolates** to every **2 dark chocolates**.
The box has 25 chocolates altogether.

a) How many are **milk chocolates**?

b) What percentage of the chocolates in a full box are dark?

4 Two people each buy **8 litres** of milk.

Julia buys 8 bottles at 54p per litre.
Sam buys two 4-litre bottles at £1·93 per bottle.

Who pays more for the 8 litres and by how much?

5 In a TV phone-in show **6700** calls were made altogether.
56% of the calls were made by females.

How many calls were made by females?

6 Three cups of coffee and two biscuits together cost **£2·65**.

One cup of coffee costs **57p**.
What is the price of **one biscuit**?

7 Dan uses **478 g** of flour.

a) Write this amount in **kilograms.**

b) How many **50 g** scoopfuls of flour can be taken
from a bag containing **0·6 kg** of flour?

8 Ahmed draws a rectangle onto paper and
measures its sides. The **perimeter** of his
rectangle is **19 cm longer** than the **width**
of his rectangle.

The **area** of the rectangle is **35 cm²**.

a) What is the **length** of his rectangle?

b) What is the **width** of his rectangle?

Solve these mixed calculations.

1 $12 \times \frac{1}{6} =$ ☐

2 $265 \times 10 =$ ☐

3 $2{\cdot}7 \times 100 =$ ☐

4 $11 \times \frac{1}{2} =$ ☐

5 $872 \times 100 =$ ☐

6 $0{\cdot}14 \times 100 =$ ☐

7 $\frac{1}{5} \div 2 =$ ☐

8 $\frac{1}{6} \div 3 =$ ☐

9 $729 \div 12 =$ ☐

10 $426 \div 18 =$ ☐

11 $729 \div 24 =$ ☐

12 $4678 \div 23 =$ ☐

13 $3{\cdot}77 \times 18 =$ ☐

14 $8{\cdot}34 \times 23 =$ ☐

15 £$36 \times 21 =$ ☐

16 $23 \times 63 \, mm =$ ☐

17 $\quad 319\,577$
$+ \quad 28\,846$
$\overline{}$

18 $24 \times \frac{1}{5} =$ ☐

19 $26\,150 \div 100 =$ ☐

20 $\frac{1}{10}$ of $7 =$ ☐

21 $15 \times \frac{1}{8} =$ ☐

22 $24 \times 18 \, kg =$ ☐

23 $13\,700 \div 1000 =$ ☐

24 $\frac{1}{8} \div 3 =$ ☐

25 $78 \times 36 \, cm =$ ☐

26 $867 \div 12 =$ ☐

27 $531 \div 24 =$ ☐

28 $867 \div 15 =$ ☐

29 $6487 \div 31 =$ ☐

30 $78{\cdot}69 \times 19 =$ ☐

31 $98{\cdot}78 \times 26 =$ ☐

32 $38 \times 42 \, l =$ ☐

33 £$76 \times 88 =$ ☐

34 $\quad 50\,020$
$- \quad 19\,509$
$\overline{}$

Percentage puzzles

The riddles below involve using some of the letters of different words to spell new ones.

1 Work out the riddle. What is the word?

> **What word am I?**
> **I am:**   the first 50% of CARPET
>
>   the middle 20% of WATER
>
>   the last $\frac{5}{6}$ of FRIDGE

2 Work out the second riddle. What is the word?

> **I am:**   the first $\frac{2}{9}$ of ADJECTIVE
>
>   the last 20% of STAND
>
>   the middle $\frac{1}{3}$ of STITCH
>
>   the last 30% of OCCUPATION

3 Work out the third riddle. What is the word?

> **I am:**   the last $\frac{3}{8}$ of ELEPHANT
>
>   the first 40% of ELBOW
>
>   the last 37·5% of ENVELOPE

4 Describe the proportion of bold letters in each word and write these as a riddle. Write each proportion as a fraction. What word do they spell?

BADGE   **SK**I   NE**TS**   LAM**B**   SH**ALL**

5 Now rewrite the same riddle using only percentages.

6 Write a riddle using these words in the same way. Use a mixture of fractions and percentages in your clues.

CATERPILLARS   CATN**AP**   **UL**TIMATE

7 Write a riddle using these words in the same way.

MATHEMATICAL   ACCID**ENTAL**   QUICKLY

8 Is it possible to write a riddle for these using only whole number percentages? Explain your answer.

SUBSET   **TRACT**OR   MULTIPLICAT**ION**

9 Write clues using fractions and percentages to make your own riddle to spell the word **UNDERSTANDING.**

10 Now make up your own riddle using only whole number percentages in your clues. Make the words in your clues as long as possible.

Series Editor
Ruth Merttens

Author Team
Jennie Kerwin and Hilda Merttens

Published by Pearson Education Limited, Edinburgh Gate, Harlow, Essex, CM20 2JE.

www.pearsonschools.co.uk

Text © Pearson Education Limited 2014
Page design and layout by room9design
Original illustrations © Pearson Education Limited 2014
Illustrated by Andy Rowland pp14–17, 19–20, 27–30, 34, 36–37, 39, 41, 47–48, 64, 75–76;
Matt Buckley pp8, 12–14, 25–26, 42, 44–45, 49–59, 61–63; Andrew Painter p47
Cover design by Pearson Education Limited
Cover illustration and Abacus character artwork by Volker Beisler © Pearson Education Limited
Additional contributions by Hilary Koll and Steve Mills, CME Projects Ltd.
First published 2014

16 15 14
10 9 8 7 6 5 4 3 2 1

British Library Cataloguing in Publication Data
A catalogue record for this book is available from the British Library

ISBN 978 1 408 27858 1

Printed in Slovakia

Acknowledgements
We would like to thank the staff and pupils at North Kidlington Primary School, Haydon Wick Primary School, Swindon, St Mary's Catholic Primary School, Bodmin, St Andrew's C of E Primary & Nursery School, Sutton-in-Ashfield, Saint James' C of E Primary School, Southampton and Harborne Primary School, Birmingham, for their invaluable help in the development and trialling of this book.

Every effort has been made to contact copyright holders of material reproduced in this book. Any omissions will be rectified in subsequent printings if notice is given to the publishers.